MW01504323

...e Face of the Other

Clara A.B. Joseph was born in India and lives in Calgary, Canada with her husband, Varghese Thekkevallyara. Her poetry has appeared in publications such as the *Toronto Review*, *Mother Earth International*, *Prosopisia: An International Journal of Poetry & Creative Writing*, *Canadian Women's Studies*, the *Journal of Postcolonial Writing*, and *Transnational Literature*.

She is the author of several academic articles and book chapters. Her book, *The Agent in the Margin: Nayantara Sahgal's Gandhian Fiction* (Wilfred Laurier UP, 2008), was nominated by the Writers' Guild of Alberta for the Wilfred Eggleston Award for Non-Fiction Prize. It also won a national Aid to Scholarly Publications Program, Canada.

Her edited books include, *Global Fissures: Postcolonial Fusions* (Rodopi, 2006), *Theology and Literature: Rethinking Reader Responsibility* (Palgrave Macmillan 2006), and special issues of the journal *World Literature Written in English* – "The Postcolonial and Globalisation" (2002) and "Rethinking the Postcolonial and Globalisation" (2002).

The Face of the Other is Clara Joseph's first book of poetry. It takes inspiration from the works of the Jewish-French master philosopher, Emmanuel Levinas, especially his ethical project of the responsibility of the self when encountering the other person.

She has a PhD in English from York University and is an associate professor of English and an adjunct associate professor of Religious Studies at the University of Calgary.

Interactive Press
The Literature Series

The Face of the Other

(A Long Poem)

Clara A.B. Joseph

Interactive Press
Brisbane

Interactive Press
an imprint of IP (Interactive Publications Pty Ltd)
Treetop Studio • 9 Kuhler Court
Carindale, Queensland, Australia 4152
sales@ipoz.biz
http://ipoz.biz/interactive-press/

First published by IP in 2016
© Clara A. B. Joseph, 2016

Printed in 12 pt Cochin.

National Library of Australia Cataloguing-in-Publication entry

Creator:	Joseph, Clara A. B., author.
Title:	The face of the other / Clara Joseph
ISBN:	9781925231359 (paperback)
Subjects:	Lévinas, Emmanuel, 1906-1995–Influence
	Philosophy–Poetry
Dewey Number:	811.6

Dedicated to George Joseph (Jr) –
my Bhaiya, *who held me tall*
for a camera shot
only the other day and,
I was two.

Acknowledgements

A Social Sciences and Humanities Research Council (SSHRC) Standard Research Grant (2011-14) supported research on the philosophy of Emmanuel Levinas, which in turn resulted in this creative project.

The title of the poem is inspired by Levinas' theory of the ethics of the face of the other.

The verses that begin, "I walk the earth that earths" is forthcoming in the *Journal of Feminist Studies in Religion* under the title, "The Other Eve."

The verses that begin, "And then the long-awaited wrinkle" is forthcoming in a revised version in the *Journal of Postcolonial Writing* under the title, "Remembering Chelva."

The last four lines of the verses that begin "Turn your eyes mildly or simply feel," are taken from T.S. Eliot's "The Love Song of J. Alfred Prufrock."

The verses that begin "On way from school" appeared in *Canadian Women's Studies 20.3* (Summer 2000): 47, under the title, "The Cart."

The last line of the verses that begin "Funny! Sure funny!" is taken from Frantz Fanon's *Black Skin, White Masks* (1967).

The cover design is the painting, titled "Redemption," by Andrew Paul (Andy's Abstract's), the abstract artist from Bangalore, India.

Ripple concentric makes shimmer face;
shape and sheen dissolve sideways into
your brain. There it now strikes
a lodging place.

You drink in a single gulp hoping
only to still your thirst, before
the breath of another breathes:
broken dreams and bruises.

Brushes lightly the suck, the lips
mimicking a lover's   kiss.
It throttles in a take of
an embrace of a singleness. Inside,

the brokenness
dances to the edge –
this life, this you,
that me in you.

Ω

Out there the fallen
leaf revives – a subtle stirring, unsettling
the space of plain air, after all was
so cordially for-

saken. It rises to this inane pull of
a one-way traffic,
lowering later to the weight of
water in a fist . . . wind, dizzy again at temporary doom.

It lingers before the good-bye at the teethed fence
in a letting go, the going after a staying,
never knowing the seeping in an oozing in
a love-like hollowing. Never knowing

me on that other side, the unseen
side of you observing the bobbing
leaf, its twirling so caught up in
a comic destiny, when I just walked away.

Ω

I walk the earth that earths
you in dust to dust to dust
to dus' dus' dus' thus Thou
should'st mark Thine image —

Thy image mocked by a pine-
apple. And serpentine
servers sweeten the dark
mother's face. No one is surprised

that I should turn
to rare voice of voiceless beasts
swishing in a slither of a swear-
word wounding my womb with

Thy curse upon my face
stuffed, the chew dripping
the dew dropping upon
my tongue in you

                in Africa,
South America,

                            Asia,
             good old Eritrea.

All to Adam's Peak.
Ascend Jews and Buddhists,
Christians, Zoroastrians,
Saracens, in search of one man's foot-

prints pressed into dust
hardened into harsh rock

where only men may bow
head, still touch ground to

slurp swish
of stream;
the sip before
the last step, before

the foot in foot,
the quenching
at my face.

Ω

Trace the word. Face
my face. Directly know what is
alterity & transcendence: I am, after all,
not God.

Feel my cheek for the alphabet, wade
into my brow, touch my lips, read in
Braille the lesson of
my dignity.

I am hiding in each p/article; I bow low in
a fearing excitement; I wait
for you knowing
you will soon stop counting.

Ω

Ces yeux blind-
folded, shoulders bared
to seeing eyes seeing
not. The half-covered face.

Glad to meet you madam
justice. Your balance hangs
from slender arms
bare. Bare. Bare.

By the rivers of Babylon
now sits the madam covered
from top to toe
in a purdah;

justice is meted with help of
ophthalmologists and dentists, allied:
eye for eye
tooth for tooth.

Pluck, pull, and banish
the name upon an unknown
face.

Is this the code of
insight, O Ammurapi?

Ω

Lift this life – pull it tight, stretch and draw
Around my arm; for the blood in my veins,
Its gush and grinding pause, the bristles on
The skin, each finger free, is otherworldly

Bliss – or so you state your own
Existence: the blue is fast spreading on sheaves
and sheaves of white with theory,
until – the midnight mockery in a single knock. Indeed.

You have been trying so hard,
lifting yourself so very high by your own boot-
strings. You are loath
to being disturbed. But.

This is simply a beckoning, a tapping
on your chest, awakening you
From your own wakening, asking you
To brush yourself away.

What you call
Transcendence is twice tripped,
Trodden like a timid shadow. Yet,
This is only me.

Ω

I thirst
mouthless, I plead
voiceless. I set my facelessness
toward Jerusalem.

Ω

Shattered shape and the glee of being
the first to catch the change, to face
the scatter, the shards by shots.
Smithereens. All is still

wonderment,
the ride up and down in
space. All is still home at four pee em. Until
the pain

beneath the sweaty school uniform,
under the reddening   shorts;

somewhere
inside
the fear –

no one might grade
the conjugated
call
voco vocamus vocas vocatis vocat vocant ...

Ω

Light lulled then lit in lines are
cheeky looks, cheekily, and Cheers! Chao!
The sudden disappearance in a ripple,
the reappearance in a lie at ease with

itself, the sweet-smiling when all the world turns
sour or insane at odd reasoning, is same as
no one is ever moving. All is like the plain
daylight in static expression. All is pain in

the black hollow of the mouth,
and all is lit on the bridge to
nowhere
for the one so fully bald, so thin.

This is someone who looks
so like something, so Picasso-like,
with only the expression of
speech.

There is nothing before the word,
nor after. In the beginning was
the word or a face,
so moving in not moving, plain water.

Ω

Eyes straining

Training on a hidden
Enemy moving
In a turbulence of breathing
A soldier piercing
With his look
Framing
Nearing
Zeroing

Breathing just once before pulling
The trigger
But breath clearing
Seeing
Revealing a woman of
The same nation indeed

Causes some hesitation

He lingering, eyeing
The shapely profile
(fear very much becomes her)
Relaxing, loosening, moving
Closer into

An increasing distance
Closing in all the same
To pull his trigger
Right into the other

Ω

A profile is silhouetted against
a latrine wall where divine messages of
love appear alongside
'f U c k.'

Feverish fingers of
some freak fumble,
then fling all over again
fresh faeces. Fly buzz

in one buzzing
burying in grooves
grooving festering
flowering

hope in a curl of golden crap.

Ω

Disheveled, dandruffed,
colored a certain shade (surely
for natural effect), and
studied from behind,
the face facing forward
daring deliberations:
dialogues with
a terrorist.

Drums
          of doom are
dhum

dhum

dhumming,

the vessels are pounding
and the blood,

does it roar in your ears?
You do not hear?
And I just said: Listen!
. . .

on the other side of you.
On the other side of you, stillness,
stealth, and a deafening silence
broken only, believe me, in defense.

On the other side of you
you do not see

the exploding line –
drenched darkness.

Gi-gi-ga-ga-grunu-grunu.
But you cannot listen for lack of
eye; cannot see with the disturbed
ear, the only defendant.
Order! Order!

And I just said: Listen!

on the other side of
you it is

me

saying

Ω

On way from school

I see an old man

Running pushing a cart

He's old and thin

Yet runs fast

Then swipes his hand

Across his arse

To fling the running shit aside

Still keeps running

To boss or home

I never know

But help he did not get.

I reach home

Am served my tiffin

I see the food, the yellow curry

Know I'll throw up

So ditch the food behind the dining-room door

The ayah might wonder for a minute

And then sweep it off.

Today I'm old

An old, old, woman

The tears it runs

Down my eyes

I swipe my hand

Across my face

To fling the running shit aside

Still keep running

To boss or home

You never know

But help I do not get.

Ω

Shook seeds and sunflowers upturned
in utter silence is
dazzle of ah beauty and age-old
sun-worship!

Who watches whom? Tell me of this daily
ritual in the garden above
lilies, hibiscus, and
the sun rising now —

descending upon sleepy flower-
heads closing in a descent and a dream
of another rising and
a blooming in dew dropping.

Who watches whom? Tell me!
Tell me before such beauty
and fade of flowers or suns; before all that,
I am.

Ω

Even the striped bush settles
After the urgent wag,
The barked at wonder, at
The spots that slithered,
Disappeared.

The questioning end of
A leap into a million leaves,
The cautious purr and the grip,
After a short while unwinds

As winged arrows take
Flight to perch at last
Directly above
The disordered nest.

That wailing one is now
Giggling at all the daily fuming.
Only you, my friend, are still twitching
Not letting me go or simply
Not letting go.

Ω

Funny! Sure funny! Funny that Fanon freaked

Out when five year old Freddie, frightened, mind you,

Said he'd seen this, mind you, clung to his mother

Like he was going to have a fit, high fever perhaps!

Poor child! He was a child, you see. A child about

This big, just this big, just a child, perhaps this big.

What did he know?! A child! But he was trembling

His head hot perhaps. Who knows? But sure he was

Scared to shit! The boy trembling like he'd seen the devil

Himself! He was scared. Plain scared! Just the sight!

What to say?! Such sights, not good for five year olds.

It sure would grow with him, waking, playing, eating, hurting

Child, hurting, hurting at school, hurting on the street

Pavements sprouting such sights! Walking like this, like this

Doing nothing, just walking with his mother, seeing sights

Simple, simple like a pigeon here, a big raven there

Pecking at crumbs of bread flung by the street vendor

Smiling at the crow, at the boy, at himself, all smiling

Shyly looking back and smiling again, our boy, this vendor

Like his Dada, red-nosed, not so tall, the plumpy kind, he

Too chubby, cheeks ruddy, so cute! The mother smiling

At her son, at the kind vendor, her cute son too doing

Nothing more than smiling, walking, he, she, they, like us …

No wonder he was so frightened!

His eyes, this big! His breath

In gasps, like a train, starting huff, puff, huff huff puff puff

Faster, faster! Then not! He'd turned cold! Icy cold! So still

His body! He wasn't moving! Not an inch! How horrible

The vision! His mother quickly grabbing his hand, his head

Shaking like he's begging it to go away or not be there

Looking him back like that, just being there to scare him

So badly his mother trying, trying, he shaking, shaking

Away the vision stopping his breathing, he shaking

Away, away! It was bad! Poor child! Breathing at last,

"Mama, see the Negro! I'm frightened!"

Ω

Rage wrinkles its brow, not so the sun in its prime

Whose molten temper remains white

In a merciless glare smooth upon those who carry

A ten-fold hell inside.

The way is short and simple.

Directly there. Authorities point with

The assurance that comes to those in broad daylight

Experienced in the art of

Subtraction.

Every soul shall taste of death; you shall surely
be paid in full your wages on the Day
of Resurrection.

There. One less each

Time.

The slip and slide of coolness relieve the chaffed

Feet made respectfully bare

In the heat and dust left behind by the beloved

Dead. Walking over their

Not-yet-forgotten-ones these bear the brunt of all

That was once-upon-a-time. They pay to etch

Upon the tombstone one full name, two dates,

Then ponder over the length of alphabets and

Brevity of an idea,

All for what they are worth –

The epitaph in

Local currency.

Let's go, child, come, take a step out

Of the wild. This stone.

Some evil jinn of Baghdad has cursed

The spot, turned it into bitter salt, from

The time when you and I walked here, and there was

No space for you.

This is no place for you.

Get up!

Around us the people fret above the eternal silence

That only lies about like slabs of stone: the well-dressed

loved ones stare back with matching resignation while

The less involved carry on,

The world briefly broken off at

The entrance to the mausoleum. Here

I've prayed to myself to

Please be rid of an abstract conception: life.

There is no universal life, only that of a bud, a kitten,

You. No capital Life.

Just its life; then, the life of a creature

Bourne out of mine in the midst of all that tea

Poured out into the Boston sea (as per your *Reader*).

At the party you were naughty, and you could still be

Told apart from the rest of my cat. You were,

My darling, utterly useless!

The black hat that raised its back like a question mark,

The black hat that brushed itself against my cheek

Dangled for one long minute from the rack until

It took one short leap,

Curled about his head, and fell asleep…. (You like that?)

It feels like yesterday that we laughed,

You happy at making me laugh, I amused at what

You had imagined upon this sight –

You were always a philosopher in your own

Right. One hand you slip into mine,

The other you point at

The grave-walkers, and the wonder

Brimming in your eyes as

You ask: Daddy, are these the resurrected ones?

Oh, how we laughed! You joining me, though

Not entirely rid of your own puzzle;

I taking your tale to

Your mother,

All our friends, your cousins; so many in

The assembly laughing; the joke

Returning, too quickly, to brighten

The tear at your

Farewell.

Let's go, child, with the black hat which,

I cannot help remembering now, you hold in

Your palm. I know it remains

Cuddled to your chest, warming

You against the cold of death.

The people drag their existence step by step

Keeping the lengthening shadow . . .

Always at their feet.

Time's up!

I'm bruised by resurrection.

Ω

I thirst

mouthless, I plead
voiceless. I set my facelessness
towards Jerusalem.

Ω

Is this the face . . .
O Helen make me immortal
with a kick, rejoins elder cousin
placing a nest of witty genitals

into little palms.
Wiggling squirrels are ever-ready to eat
a human child, but transform instead
into one sturdy snake
live, lifting itself for a kiss.
                Knees lock and a non-kick.
Eyes daze in sudden sleepiness.
And an awkward foaming
at the lip is
hello helen.

And my father's face freaks out when broken-
winged angels, toothless 'n old, pound
day and night at his door
shut tight.

Ω

And then the long-awaited wrinkle
Like a twinkle appears above
The now naughty nose, rounded. The slender lines –
One, two, three, four... and the jaunty eye
Made up with khol and castor oil
The night before this rendezvous. We meet to
Each other's laughter of silver tumblers
Pealing past stony steps. We can smell
Each other's skin; we take
The tribal step, in time, and move
Closer to each other and
God is passing through.

Ω

For the world is full
of lies and lines about
seeing and dying.
Thou shal't not

look upon the face of God
and live.
Shalt not! Shalt not!

Seeing sears the very skin
in a knowing; it is a gnawing of
a wholeness upon a metal plate
or on water without a stirring.

It is an un-breaking of reflective power
in a boastful bidding where
someone is losing.

Sought in a sight and studied by rote
in a rendezvous or upon that first heat of
an only meet, the truth of the fact is: what is read
cannot be unread, the known unknown, and never the seen
unseen. Thy gaze whips

                    across my face.
Thou hath defaced.

Ω

The world is bloating with
the bursting self. It will break out,
like banging from bombed beds; It accumulates
itself, like the ooze of oil
taken.

Why else the murder of
Blacks
Jews
Gypsies
Natives, Arabs?
Years have passed, ….
and all is seared with
trade; reared, smeared with
success; and wears the invader's brand
and style:
the land was always
empty, the sycamore fit
for pulp.

In spite of this, another is
not dead; there lives
the dignity of persons
deep down things; and though
the flash and flicker off
the mixed West went oh, today, at
the brown boarder eastward, blossoms —
because the Other moves with
mind
and soul, and
ah! such visage.

Ω

stone split swift shake tremble and
the crowd in righteousness after
one buttocked breasted
swaying from hand to hand to

feet lifting to the pull, falling to
the push
ripping unskirting
spitting bleeding spraying

splaying displaying exerting excreting
growling and
she is praying
to the gods who are continuing –

scissors snip snip snip and pliers-nip off
shameless nipples and someone is shocked
breasts are bleeding.
He puts a full-stop before

she is jerked to a standing
she begins the arriving exodus
homeward in forty years at last
falling dragging dozing

dancing when oiled limbs lit flare
agony is fearing searing
crumbling of form and face
and all is sentenced to sheer

suicidal ashes.

Ω

Blood-drenched babes like lambs, calves, or cubs are
like the naked face exposed
to an ambitious claw, a parched beak, or a gentle break
upon a well-hidden wall of stone.

Surely such fragility is least becoming,
such weakness is blameworthy,
and the exposed face has asked,
no doubt, to be eaten.

Ω

You found last night
night's black mare,
reign of darkness' demon,
donned-dined-doomed
a face, in its spreading on
the now flat screen beneath it
without air, yet expanding as wide,
how it flowed in
a flight of no escape
in its despair; again,
one last attempt,
as hands must have clung clumsily on
deadened air: the wave of
a palm
rebuffed the filthy blast.
Your eye in seeking strained
for terrain, —
the proof of,
the mapping of
the win.

Rude success and victory
and war, oh,
sand,
oil, won here
accomplished! AND
the breath that escaped
from me then, sounds
in your ear, ten times more loud,
more drawn,
dear child!

This is all normal:
to invade land crush the face
clean, with policies that
squeak; yours truly, skinned for soil,
democratically bombed.⁻

Ω

And yet. And yet. The cry arises from
the stone where man and beast have gone
to prey, when one lonely prayer orders
the stay

to an obligation enunciated

in the face that is

the eye un-shut is much obliged;
and the un-dined mouth latches shut?

Ω

ten kilograms of chains suffice for feet
and faces you shall never meet
for there are no more enquiries
at the quarries

where more than five are held
in their respective places,
slamming shoulders and dawn's shudder shook off
wet of working sweat relieving
a late night's sweltering heat

relieving the rising worth of so much
more to pay off in debt to
the stone-hearted,
the major cost of weld and iron
and the shackle worsening to
the thousands added
like the count of a cunning zero
at a neat sum's envied end

and that is when it was
time to leave the paid debt
when the lords touched their feet
in a mock salutation and welded
lives to rock, they lived
into the mettle growing
at their every strike, loading
the plying lorries with granite
cubes

when the zeroes multiplied
weighing more than the loaded blocks (all so perfect)
wives and daughters celebrated
independence day
and night upon their backs

but again hands rise
like a chorus
hiss of flesh cutting the quarry wind
grip tightening
at the descent

and the mindless explosion proclaims
all that they know is to
crush stone.

Ω

Good morning
the many named,
the mannered ways,
the already moulded
minds in a meeting of
a face. Permit
the cracking in
the simple greeting.

Give way. Dissolve
yours.

Namasté!

Ω

Or open wide your eyes or shut
them to reveal the heart of
God beating an image
to the rhythm of my feet

treading the classrooms
of your learning-to-unlearn my poverty
in you

or

hear me listening
see me seeing

You still out-beating
the missing beat
of my tired feet

battered
following.

Ω

Push, press, and prick and find even
the hardening face is bleeding.
Tears begin to curl around
distractions worth one
whole dime.

The disturbing sniffle,
the filth of another's fluid, these and more
snuffle nation-speak, whence

gushes forth
God's semantics before
a stranger
                    broken.

Ω

Chicken legs torn apart reveal
the beginning
of pubic hair before the rush of
things and motion.

All

                    is

such

forced

rhythm and no one is sleeping.
All are wide awake as
in a train chanting,
                    watching

the baring over
the spread-eagled, the lowering
with rigid mastery, hard as ever,
breaking through form, through
flesh

the weight
            and push
of someone   so   big as
                a father,   uncle –   all is terror
in a stranger's nearness in
                strange places, plundering
breath

just cannot understand why

no one is saving.
    Under
so much

    weight
    and hurt is
      lost speech.

Not a single one remembers
what lies beyond

chicken legs.

Ω

The dark brown of the mouse

scuttling between the railway tracks

is taken, is taken by the slow moving figure ahead

clad in a dead crow's flap

trailing its tattered ends. This one is

talking to herself, or so it seems, to

someone walking just behind

not comprehending the muttering or

the wild gesturing that accompany

perhaps some mighty thought.

Another is squatting,

illegally asking for change of

oil-boomers in suits marching

past the tobacco shop, heading

toward the Bow River where they will dream

of fresh air and nature, even as they meander between

crazy bike-riders and, alas, here too, the pan-handlers.

The pan-handlers do not own

a single pan. They simply cup their palm,

cup their palm and stretch out to

passers-by who have trouble understanding

from where shoots out this hand of man.

But the figure ahead does not ask of another,

only continues her slow pace until

she reaches the restaurant door where

she lingers, adjusts her cloak as if she still were wearing

a finer dress; then to everyone's surprise,

enters, only to be pushed out hastily by none

other than the place's owner who either fails to recognize

her or cannot stand to lose his

elite clientele. Back on the road she is

laughing. Back on the road she slowly begins

her dance. Her silence disappears with her

clothes that soon lie strewn all over,

all over the street center where she keeps up

her shuffle to the tune of amused folk

and the angry honk of

trains and cars, all

stopped in their track by

her naked feet,

until the law intervenes to

talk reason, talk reason into the dancing

woman, and she throws right back,

right back, every cloak pressed into

her waving arms, she throws right back

her silence.   Did they arrest

       the one who broke
your peace?

Ω

Wet-licked and morning'd is
the career-set face eating of dew
dense damp and a sudden breeze in
a single swallow of a wind unscheduled.

Wind-fattened and waked out again
is last night's bitterness,
the panic of the day before,
the bomb-burst of a sure tomorrow

and this stillness in the one
lying,
lying still,
still lying;

you do not yet know
what is lying in
a face so cold.

Ω

Twig-limbs scurried eagerly: a caterpillar at
its best – fearful and set for
full flight. The master's eyes
bore into shoulders and the brick
laid rises
speedily.

Tattered trousers all but
slip
the thin torso
tightened to stave off
hunger. The gruel

mixed in mother's morning
milk learning to last
the slow stop and
slide of a sun
at last setting for
the very young brick-layer.

Yet ten times stopped well after
it is time to go, means –
there is more
in store in
those eyes that bore all day into
shoulders and bricks.

In spite of all, after
months,

at last, and

finally

the bricks are
declared laid,
the wall
built, and its height is
loudly proclaimed as sufficient
into such a hopeful little face.

Ten times more for tasks
the caterpillar leaps
so eagerly, with
so much glee, until

asked the reason for such
immodesty – so much noise,
who was reason for such show of
teeth, such wild use of
eye?! Someone made to throw
a stone. And the caterpillar
left, wings turning quickly heavy.
Tears added salt to the late night gruel.

Next day and the next
the insect roamed
the vicinage of
the new great wall. A tender
hook extended to feel

the eternity of this wide range of
still fresh beauty, when

the master's eye bore into
shoulders and bricks,
demanding an immediate
explanation for this
evil presence.

The tender hooks joined in
fearful respect, then
extended as if for

pay.
The master's eye flicked
a slight order.
And then?

All is red or simply dead.
The gods must all be
caged.

Ω

that is exactly why verses stretch
across the rails leading away
from the funeral hut
discarding the unwieldy
tears, nasal dribble, sounds,

the perfumed dead's perfume
lingering after the dismissal and
the howling of the dead's stubborn
after the hushing

    derail

        your stanza

      Ω

Almost. Then a recovering
in good old-fashioned way:

the hat removed from
a casket
placed right back upon
the wig above a thinning head and the shroud,
the coat rather,
stiffened corpse-like,
starched or straightened rather

and the smile carefully laid
to rest above the stony chin

is now ready
now ready steady
to be greeted.

Ω

The air is eager though all too wet
when stubborn fig trees spread their skirts
this side of the highway wall. I watch in awe

yet cannot speak to you who own this wonderland.
The wind is scolding when all was still
until some pleats are pushed off this side of
the highway wall; the trains that warmed

those trims now pass us both; they pass us by.
The silence has spread, the pines have pierced
the contours of our mutual fear, have turned
to dust for wind and air both sides of the highway wall.
I lick my lips with your fame. Do you know

my name?

Ω

Turn your eyes mildly or simply feel,
An apothecary preparing to heal
When the aging sun is ready
To temporarily die
Like those who live believing
In eternity;
See
Or touch, cut through the wetness
Of fog,
Past the dancing dew, known to every
Dog, and grasped
In fierce contemplation of avaricious design
To claim popular balance
Of *ying* and *yang*
Regardless of anything right
Or wrong. Never ask,

'Why?'
Touch.
See.

The Old Man leans amidst bearded
Clouds, reaches out
A still muscular hand to create
With a single touch.

The golden sun that rubs
Its forehead against the lazy buds,
The golden sun that rubs its nose
On the awakened petals
Scolds in fiery youth

At noon, repents over
The dying grass, struggles
With closing lids,
Fading vistas,
Bursts past the waters in
One last attempt, and learning
The world has had its fill,
Drew night's blanket over,
Set.

If there will be time enough
For the golden sun that wanders
Into all spaces, poking
Its chin into everyone's business;
There will be time,
There will be time
To prepare a face to meet
The faces that you meet.

Ω

Prepare the perplexed brow and eye,
Paint the lip, line the chin with
The right shade of sin to
Meet the myriad faces.

The bells have tolled:
One tells of readiness in
A single stripping, another
Stifles the scream, the last one philosophizes

While a seventeen year old is told
She will soon be a cab-driver's wife,
And is excited.

When, O when will you marry me?
Soon. Soon. Says the driver busy now
Taking a seventeen year old would-be-bride
For a ride.

Ten times in the back of his car,
Twenty in tenements
With broken bottles and fifteen others like him,
(As witnesses to his word)

Before she begins to wonder
          And, whimpering, checks with the groom-to-be —
What is going on? Something about prostitutes
Makes her check the dictionary, reminding
                    It has been so long since she's been
to school;
              what with all the wedding plans….

The open dictionary is enough though;
Her mother marches her to the civic guardians,
The police, who find it all so amusing and jeer
Until both have disappeared, turned a full corner.

Day by day the dread of
                    deeds done
To her
dawns
                    a little more, pushes vomit
Up her   throat
at the memory of
                    a touch,
Wrecks

                                                    what
            little
                              sleep
she steals upon the brutal

bed.

The police send for her again, usual procedure they say,
To hear the minute details one more time:
Where exactly, how tightly, deeply,
Didn't it all feel so good really? Tell the truth!

The spittle
                    foams at both edges of her mouth
Dribbles   onto her blouse. Her mother wipes
Hers own away   at the very nick of time. Once more
They turned the corner clean,
                              noting

Nothing had been written, no record taken
Of all the truth that had again been told.

          when
                    temple bells toll in

midday crowd, seventeen year old   twists
          mother's
          sari
          sturdy
          rope

loop tightens
                         kicks

study

                    chair.

                    Ω

Never say, there was no chair, they squat
Over there. Squatters too can climb and kill,
Taunt you with their dangling pain when
You have almost turned away:

One red and yellow – a brush of brown
So ready for the picking, then the packing,
And the final profiting, if you have taken
No note, until all is ripened, just before

The rotting sets in, and you are simply afraid.
So, you say, in spite of the currency and the coins,
You say, after you have rested your tea
Where a c.d. should be, they . . . they . . . squat.

You test your irritability with another sip;
You soothe it with the tip of your tongue,
And turn around in search of
Something to still its need to sting.

So, you say, after you have bitten into a donut,
After you have admired the exact C
You have just created,
There is no chair . . .

As you watch it leap out
Of your mouth, or your heart
Really, and yet not go anywhere
Further than your own thought.

And you have brushed the crumbs
Off the ergonomic keyboard,
Between the letter U and I,
And you say again, they . . .

❊ ❊ ❊

They squat, alright! They squat right upon
Your brain where the chain is (why?)
Too tight. They squat you like a fly
At the moment that they die.

Why else the rested tea, the stammer,
And the words like a ruthless hammer?
Why this perseverance in minute detail
Of the native place of the other?

Ω

Time ticks
            ticks
ticks; time will
tell if
            you can
wrestle the   other nestled in
your   mother

Ω

All this is public knowledge.
All is done in broad daylight where the killin'
Youth and the not-so-young-still-smart-lookin'
Gather in one display   of unity

Against three men who look like vermin
Already. You cannot bear
The digital proof all over

Again. Please do not forget
The return of the hammer
On heads and living bodies;

Its rhythm like the universal clock,
Not missing
A single
Beat.

The barely lifting palms
Begging for a moment
To only

Breathe.

The voice so unmanly,

Girlish, you might say,
Coming from grown-up men sprawling,
Plainly asking not to hurt
The triple-kicked face

Where blood not just then
But later
Begins to ooze
As if from only the black head of

The now dead, when the killin' youth
And the not-so-young-still-smart-lookin' turn
Toward a not so smart lookin' youth
A teenager really, and shove him

O what *maza*!

Shove him into their midst and begin
The kickin'
And the hammerin'
And the hammerin'
And the hammerin'
And he . . . the fallin'
And the beggin'

Ω

Then the squeakin'
Before the dyin'

Ω

Not!
Not!
Not!

Sweet this one
Sweet this one
Because I can

Sweet this one because
I can hear her into
Speaking

Sweet this one because
I can hear her into
Spear and into breaking

Ω

If you cannot see the face, don't fret.
Simply spread your shawl upon my shoulder
Where the sun sucks at my sweat
Somewhere inside, then stand back and watch

Me
Run to you and back. Watch me
Kiss my mother goodbye, wipe away
My father's tears

Dripping with mortality. Watch me
Kill my cows, cook into a curry,
And feed my people at the last supper,
Upon the fuel of my own plough.

✿ ✿ ✿

Your shawl is still upon my back.
I wear it tightly across my chest,
In a snuggle of a sleep,
The costume of your awakening.

Ω

So. Come on and call in my face
your God and account
for your high theology: scrawl your notes
right on my nose and read in my (shady) eye

'thou shalt not kill'; learn your abc
d, e, f, g, h, i, j, k, l, m, n, o, p. Lmnopqrst, uvwxyz,
be still and see that it is me
you have just bought along with
the bag of books,
every drop of me carefully caught,
distilled off the bobbing leaf, bottled

drenching the text
into tatters, into meanings
multiple, making the deconstructed
word judge.

Handle with care
the sun arriving upon me
on wings of a healing,
wings covering top to toe
me from you.

I thirst
mouthless, I plead
voiceless. I set my facelessness
towards Jerusalem.

O Jerusalem, Jerusalem, how I long…!
Go! Gather the brokenness,

The breath in all that blood,
Sense in the silence of a moment.

Find me! In all that fumbles
and in freakish guises
where vermin is venerated find
the glow of my morrow.

Speak! I command thee
speak! The speech stilled to
a perfect silence at the final
listening.

And you have plucked
and now hold between your thumb
and un/kindness the budding of
a being; that is not you

who have not rested
a pinky on a frail forget-me-not yet
know the flutter and the fade,
the whimper of a toddler dew.

Re-turn the turned nape upon a hearing
of a crying, carried carelessly in a crumble
in a coat upturned; goggled; top-hatted.
Return to the one you just scarred.

To the ashes of a by-gone narrative
ripped out of someone's pages,
to the scorched skull and the betrayed limb,
in an age-old greeting, return.

And hold ever so gently the cub
between your teeth; lick dry the newborn
calf off fear. Bow low before
the Word.

Only never say you do not know
the worth of a word, that there are
no cutters in your countryside or worse –
point away at five more like me.

I know. The word that just fled my mouth totters
at the edge of you, commanding
without a single rhyme.
Thou shalt!

It is bleeding in a pleading (forgive the rhyme)
calling you,
yes you, to please be
by my side.

And to that end of all things you shall
arrive as "I"
(omega)

Ω

Ω

Made in the USA
Middletown, DE
25 September 2016